U-2 PLANES

BY DENNY VON FINN

EPIC

BELLWETHER MEDIA · MINNEAPOLIS, MN

EPIC

EPIC BOOKS are no ordinary books. They burst with intense action, high-speed heroics, and shadows of the unknown. Are you ready for an Epic adventure?

This edition first published in 2014 by Bellwether Media, Inc.

Library of Congress Cataloging-in-Publication Data

Von Finn, Denny.
U-2 planes / by Denny Von Finn.
pages cm. – (Epic: military vehicles)
Includes bibliographical references and index.
Summary: "Engaging images accompany information about U-2 planes. The combination of high-interest subject matter and light text is intended for students in grades 2 through 7"–Provided by publisher.
Audience: Ages 6-12.
ISBN 978-1-60014-944-3 (hbk. : alk. paper)
1. U-2 (Reconnaissance aircraft)–Juvenile literature. I. Title.
UG1242.R4V56 2014
358.4'583–dc23
2013003496

Printed in the United States of America, North Mankato, MN.

The photographs in this book are reproduced through the courtesy of the United States Department of Defense.
A special thanks to the following for additional photos: Photo 12/ Collection Bernard Crochet/ Alamy, pp. 4-5;
Lee Jin-man/ AP Images, p. 6; Ted Carlson, pp. 14-15, 19, 20; Phillip Wallick/ Age Fotostock, p. 11; Vincent Laforet/

TABLE OF CONTENTS

U-2 Planes

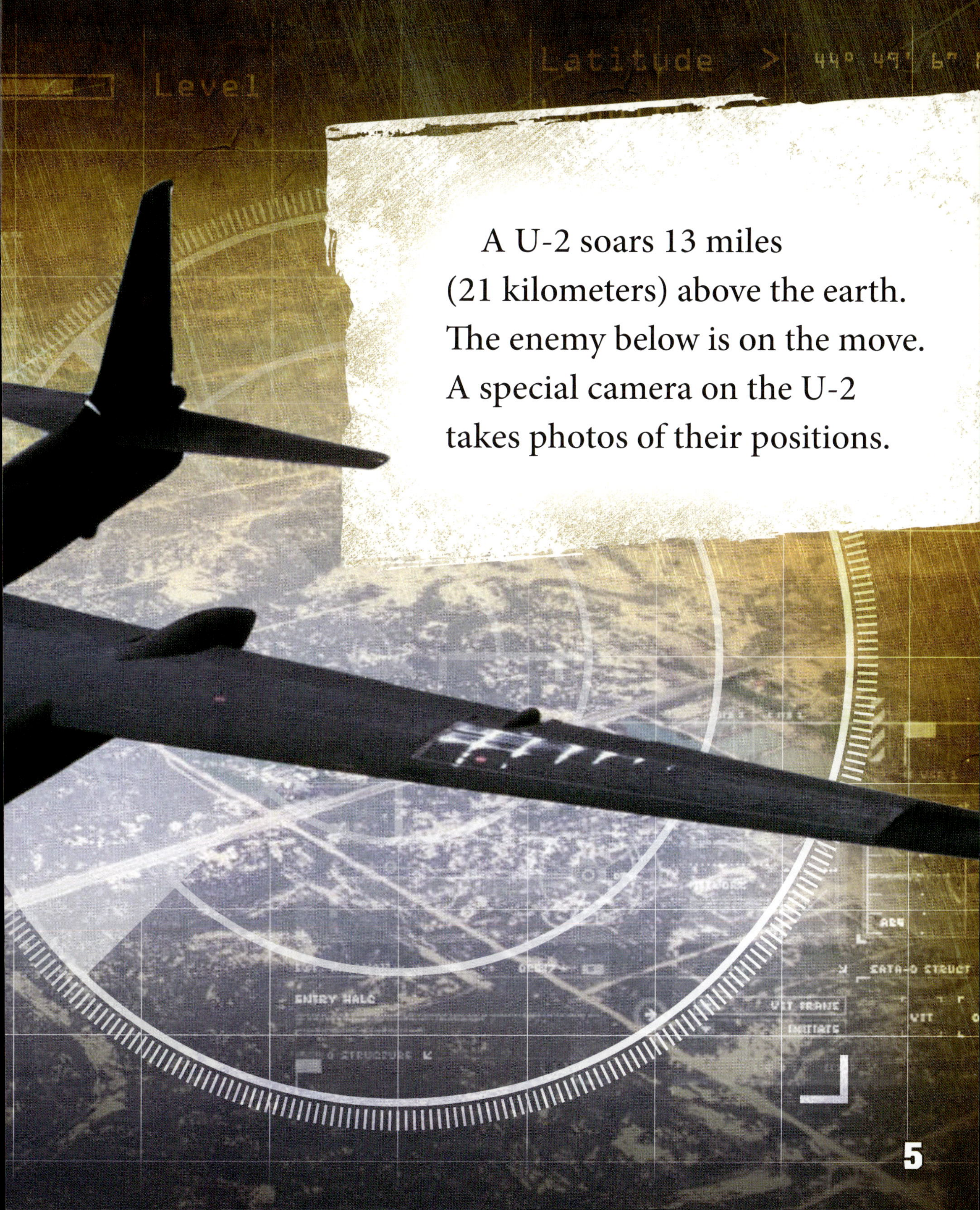

A U-2 soars 13 miles (21 kilometers) above the earth. The enemy below is on the move. A special camera on the U-2 takes photos of their positions.

Spy Plane Fact

A U-2 can carry enough fuel to stay in flight for 12 hours. This lets pilots fly far into enemy air space.

The U-2's **mission** is complete. The pilot turns for home. The enemy does not know it has been photographed.

Parts and Crew

The U-2 is a U.S. Air Force spy plane. Its **recon** missions help soldiers on the ground. It flies too high for enemies to see.

Spy Plane Fact

U-2s fly so high that pilots must wear space suits.

The U-2 has a powerful camera. It takes clear photos from a high **altitude**. The U-2 also uses **radar** to gather **intelligence**.

A long nose and narrow wings help the U-2 reach high altitudes. They also make the U-2 hard to fly.

Spy Plane Fact

A U-2 needs help landing. A car races behind the plane. Its driver radios instructions to the pilot.

A U-2 has two wheels between its wings. Two more wheels are near its **jet engine**. The U-2 tips to one side after landing.

Spy Plane Fact

One wing drags on the ground after a U-2 lands. Metal plates protect the wings as the U-2 slows down.

U-2 MISSIONS

Spy Plane Fact

A U-2 was shot down over the Soviet Union in 1960. The pilot parachuted to safety but was held there for almost two years.

The U-2 was first built during the **Cold War**. It flew famous missions over Cuba and the Soviet Union.

Spy Plane Fact

Hurricane Katrina hit the U.S. in 2005. U-2 planes flew over Louisiana to photograph the damage.

NEW ORLEANS, LOUISIANA

U-2s have flown in the **War on Terror**. They are even used to take photographs of **natural disasters**.

U-2s have gathered intelligence for more than 50 years. Their brave pilots fly high above the earth to keep soldiers and **civilians** safe.

VEHICLE BREAKDOWN: U-2 PLANE

Used By:	U.S. Air Force
Entered Service:	1956
Length:	63 feet (19.2 meters)
Height:	16 feet (4.8 meters)
Maximum Takeoff Weight:	40,000 pounds (18,144 kilograms)
Wingspan:	105 feet (32 meters)
Top Speed:	more than 410 miles (660 kilometers) per hour
Range:	7,000 miles (11,265 kilometers)
Ceiling:	above 70,000 feet (21,336 meters)
Crew:	1
Weapons:	none
Primary Mission:	high-altitude recon

GLOSSARY

altitude—distance above sea level

civilians—people who are not in the military

Cold War—a conflict between the United States and Soviet Union that lasted from 1945 to 1991; it was called the "Cold War" because there were no direct battles between the two countries.

intelligence—information about an enemy's position, movements, or weapons

jet engine—a powerful engine that pushes a plane forward

mission—a military task

natural disasters—major events that occur in nature; hurricanes, floods, and earthquakes are types of natural disasters.

radar—a system that uses radio waves to locate targets

recon—a type of mission that involves gathering information about the enemy

War on Terror—a war led by the United States to stop organized groups from performing acts of violence; the War on Terror began in 2001.

TO LEARN MORE

At the Library

Braulick, Carrie A. *U.S. Air Force Spy Planes.* Mankato, Minn.: Capstone Press, 2007.

David, Jack. *U-2 Planes.* Minneapolis, Minn.: Bellwether Media, 2008.

Shea, Therese. *Spy Planes.* New York, N.Y.: Gareth Stevens Publishing, 2013.

On the Web

Learning more about U-2 planes is as easy as 1, 2, 3.

1. Go to www.factsurfer.com.

2. Enter "U-2 planes" into the search box.

3. Click the "Surf" button and you will see a list of related Web sites.

With factsurfer.com, finding more information is just a click away.

INDEX

THREAT DETECTED